BLESS
THE
EARTH

BLESS
THE
EARTH

A Collection of Poetry for
Children to Celebrate and
Care for Our World

EDITED BY

JUNE COTNER and NANCY TUPPER LING

ILLUSTRATED BY

KEUM JIN SONG

For my four grandchildren:
Shay, Weston, Kailen, and Camille

~JUNE

For all my writer friends:
The Magic Story Makers, Wind in the Cypress,
and the Fine Line Poets

Soli Deo Gloria

~NANCY

CONTENTS

A NOTE ABOUT THIS BOOK

"It's so fragile." These were the words of ninety-year-old actor William Shatner, as he recently observed Earth from outer space aboard a Blue Origin rocket. Even without heading into space, we can still recognize the vital importance of protecting our planet. Certainly, climate change and environmental awareness are at the forefront of topics that parents and teachers discuss with children. Still, how do we begin to treasure this place we call home?

Through universal prayers of gratitude and earth-related inspirational poems, *Bless the Earth* encourages families to celebrate the miracle of our world. It also offers another dimension of caring that is often overlooked—a spiritual one. This anthology knits together humanity, the environment, and spirituality in an engaging way.

The final section, titled "Caring for Our World," is a call to action, as illustrated by the first stanza of the poem by Susanne Wiggins Bunch "It's Up to Us":

> Yes, it's up to you and me
> to care for the gifts we're given,
> the earth, the sky, the sea.

Truly our hope is that this collection will help parents and children not only cherish Earth but also become stewards of all its beauty.

With gratitude,

June and Nancy

BLESS THE EARTH

Bless the Earth, our faithful friend,
her mountain range and river bend,
her forest green and canopy,
the hidden world of bended trees.

Bless the Earth, her morning song,
hold it close, it lingers on,
like tender trails that cross the sky—
the paths of bee and butterfly.

Both spiraled shell and painted wing,
these are the gifts that each day brings.
Bless the Earth, both land and sea,
she means the world to you and me.

Nancy Tupper Ling

DREAMS
AND PRAYERS
FOR MY
WORLD

DREAMS FOR MY WORLD

My world is little
It's a kiss and a hug
It's a walk outside
Or watching a bug.

My life is simple
It's eat, sleep and play
It's love and laughter
All through the day.

I want to be kind
I want to be good
To treat everybody
Just like I should.

Your world is huge
Like the sky and the trees
Like mountains and beaches
And rivers and seas.

Take care of your world
Protect what you see
So when I'm grown up
It's still there for me.

Barbara J. Mitchell

HELLO, EARTH!

It's your children.
Some of your children—
the human ones.
We have been studying you, Earth,
but we long to learn more.

We want to ask you
a few questions.
We want to
tell you our dreams
and wishes.

Can you hear us,
Earth?

Joyce Sidman

10

FOR A CHILD

EXCERPT

Your friends shall be the Tall Wind,
The River and the Tree;
The Sun that laughs and marches,
The Swallows and the Sea.

Your prayers shall be the murmur
Of grasses in the rain;
The song of wildwood thrushes
That makes God glad again.

Fannie Stearns Davis

12

A CHILD'S LULLABY FOR EARTH

Darkness falls,
Creatures call,
The people's prayers are said.
God is singing a lullaby
While earth prepares for bed.

Stars are lit,
The moon's face glows,
Bedtime stories are read.
God is singing a lullaby
While earth prepares for bed.

Barn owls hoot,
And crickets chirp,
As nighttime hush is spread.
God is singing a lullaby
While earth prepares for bed.

Dew drops fall,
Soft petals close,
Sweet dreams fill sleepy heads.
God is singing a lullaby
While earth prepares for bed.

Susanne Wiggins Bunch

DEAR CREATOR

Every color of the rainbow
Across forests, hills and seas
Rich with textures, sounds and smells
Taking care of creatures' needs
Here is home, our precious planet

Dear Creator,
    grant us Peace,
        your greatest gift.

Charlotte Sheer

BRAVO, WORLD!

Clouds make a movie.
Leaves dance a ballet.
Flowers paint a picture.
Cicadas chirp a symphony.
Spider writes a poem.
Squirrels stage a play.
Wind sings a solo.
Rain taps a rap.
And as for me,
I clap and shout, "Bravo!"

Barbara Younger

WONDER

Have you seen—
the see-through wing of a buzzing bee,
the perfect hinge of a cricket's knee,
the scoot-and-sinch of an inchworm's inch,
the dangling nest of a yellow finch?
All these tiny, wonderful things.

Can you believe—
the thunderous crash of a wave on the shore,
the *swish* and *swoosh* of a mighty wind's roar,
steep mountains that climb beyond the clouds' white,
clouds, like mountains, flashing radiant light,
spiraling galaxies, orderly grace,
a growing universe, expanding space?
All these enormous, brilliant things.

Have you seen it?
Can you believe?
The big and the small?
And a God who knows
us
in the middle of it all?

Amanda Smith

MAGIC BOX

This box is full of green leaves and clouds,
and pretty things;
soft, soft echoes from wonderland.

I am adding smiling moon,
whispered breeze,
and quiet wings,
to give you our dreams
in a handful of songs.

Ramnath Subramanian

THINK LIKE A RIVER

Think like a river.
Dream like the sky.
Drift like an eagle
That circles on high.

Breathe like the wind
That calls from the trees.
Ride like a wave
That caresses the seas.

Sleep like a secret
That whispers the night.
Wake like a wish
That warms you with light.

Charles Ghigna

I LOVE TO WONDER!

I am always wondering . . .
Why is the sky so blue?
How does the moon get so big?
Where does a river go?
Do ocean waves ever stop?

I am always wondering . . .
Why does my cat purr?
How does the bee make honey?
Where do birds go at night?
Do turtles travel far?

I am always wondering . . .
Why do I have dreams?
Where do my tears come from?
How does my hair grow?
Do animals smile like I do?

I am always wondering . . .
I love to wonder!

Judy Ackley Brown

EARTH,
SEA,
AND SKY

EARTH SPEAKS

Earth speaks:
I am here.
I have always been
and always will be.
Walk into my arms,
feel my breath,
love me
as you would a friend.

Corrine De Winter

22

THINK TENDERLY OF ME

INSPIRED BY EMILY DICKINSON

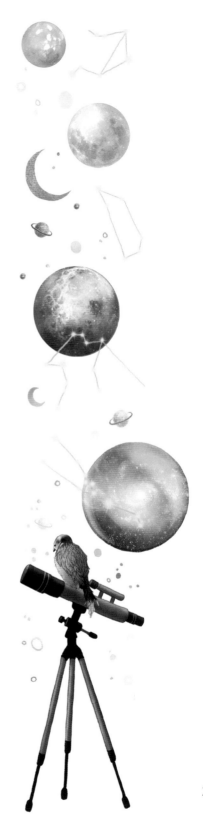

I am a rock,
a tough, gigantic sphere.
I am everywhere—far and near.

Inside, I am a fiery, melted ball.
Outside, I am a thick, protective crust.
I share my strength with you.

I am your precious planet,
your brilliant shining star,
but I am fragile.

Think tenderly of me.

Carol Murray

23

STONY WONDERS

Silky smooth in my hand,
Tiny rocks, playful sand.

Flat stones skim across the lake,
Pebbles cause a rippled wake.

Climb on top rugged boulders
Sturdy, strong like Daddy's shoulders.

Soaring peaks in azure sky,
Towering mountains, reaching high.

Rocky earth, floats in space
Among the stars with poise and grace.

Nancy Engler

24

HARD TO BELIEVE

When you walk on a desert
with sand all around
or climb up a mountain
a mile above ground
or sail on an ocean
where beaches abound,
it's hard to believe
that our planet is round.

Aileen Fisher

Night comes to the desert all at once,
as if someone turned off the light.

Joyce Carol Oates

25

INCREDIBLE CREATION

A leaf,
a tree,
a hive,
a bee.

A star
at night.
The sun's
bright light.

The sea,
a wave,
a bear,
a cave.

A bird
in flight,
and snow
soft white.

Each day
born new,
the grass,
the dew.

Amazing things,
great and small.
The LORD above
made them all!

Jill Noblit MacGregor

26

MAGICAL FOREST

Listen, do you hear
the hush of the forest?
Like a grand cathedral,
every leaf welcomes me,
every tree sparkles
with magic.

Corrine De Winter

Between every two pines is
a doorway to a new world.

John Muir

RAINFOREST SYMPHONY

God created a symphony,
under a leafy tent of green,
where steady beats of raindrops drum
on a hot and humid scene.

With the rainforest orchestra,
nature's music takes the stage
as God composes melodies
creatures love to sing and play.

High in tall trees, bright toucans sound
with birdsong all their own,
while crickets in tuxedo black
play along in rhythmic tone.

Loud insects buzz while tree frogs yelp
as they offer noisy praise
for beautiful flower dancers
on stems that bend and sway.

Wide winding rivers roar and gush.
Monkeys chatter in broad leaf trees.
Leopards growl while on the hunt.
Nature blends their harmonies.

The rainforest plays this masterpiece,
this song of earth's refrain,
"Treat me well so I'll endure
to play for you again."

Susanne Wiggins Bunch

28

LIFE CYCLE

The Stream
becomes
the River
becomes
the Root
becomes
the Tree
becomes
the Bird
becomes
the Sky
becomes
the Sun
becomes
the Cloud
becomes
the Rain
becomes
the Stream

Charles Ghigna

30

I AM THE EARTH

I love this gray. I love
this water, this cool.
I am the Earth and I long
for heaven's sweet rain.
I am green, I sprout. These
are my trees, my bushes, my blooms.
I love this gray. I love
this water, this cool.

Janine Canan

The sea is as near as we come to another world.

Anne Stevenson

31

THE SEA'S TREASURES

In swept the sea
With a swirl and a swish,
It shimmered and whispered,
'Choose what you wish.'

And the sea showed its treasures
At the edge of the shore,
Shining bright pebbles
And shells by the score.

Long ribbons of seaweed
That shone gold and red,
'I'll share them, I'll share,'
The sea softly said.

Daphne Lister

INSIDE A SHELL

Inside a shell
There is the whisper of a wave.

Inside a feather
There is the breath of a breeze.

Inside an ember
There is the memory of a flame.

Inside a rock
There is the murmur of a mountain.

Inside a well
There is the echo of a wish.

Inside a seed
There is the promise of a flower.

John Foster

33

EVERYDAY WONDERS

Life around is on the go.
Seas obey, they ebb and flow.
Sun shines bright, moonlight glows.
Flowers bud, bloom and grow.
Rain pours down from dark gray clouds.
Lightning cracks with thunder loud.
Birds build nests, then lay their eggs.
Newborn fawn on wobbly legs.
Spider spins a lacy web.
Nimble goat on mountain ledge.
Wonders everywhere are found,
in sky, and sea, and on the ground.

Jill Noblit MacGregor

GOD THE ARTIST

EXCERPT

God, when you thought of a pine tree,
How did you think of a star?
How did you dream of the Milky Way
To guide us from afar.

Angela Morgan

PURPLE

The thought of you delights me
as I look up in the sky;
I see you in the rainbow
through seagulls flying by . . .

I see you in the flower,
I see you in the tree,
And sometimes there you are
in the sparkles on the sea.

Thank You, God, for purple
and the joy it brings to me;
I see you everywhere I look
And wow!
        . . . the bumble-bee!

Fanny M. Levin

36

SINGING STARS

INSPIRED BY JOB 38:7

In the majestic morning sky
a twinkling symphony
serenades the galaxies

A choir echoes
through the Milky Way
A blessed song
created in splendor and awe

The stars sing together
The stars sing to us.

Keri Biron

IF I COULD SEE THE SKY

If I were a bird
I would fly like an eagle
Through the sweet summer sky
All day long.

But one day I will fly
To the moon and the sun.
All day long
I will not stop
Until I get to God.

Baby in a cradleboard
Riding safe
In the sky.

Jillian Pappan, age 10, Omaha Tribe of Nebraska

38

BEDTIME

If crickets sing
    or nighthawks cry,
If branches sway
    or oceans sigh,
If raindrops
    polka-dot the sky,
Lie in bed
    and close your eyes.
Listen to their lullabies.

Michelle Heidenrich Barnes

I SEE THE MOON

I see the moon,
and the moon sees me,
God bless the moon,
and God bless me!

Author unknown

41

DAY IS DONE

Day is done,
Gone the sun
From the lake,
From the hills,
From the sky.
Safely rest,
All is well!
God is nigh.

Author unknown

42

ALL
CREATURES,
BIG AND
SMALL

MORNING SONG

It begins with a whisper.
Over meadow, robin stirs.
Feathers rustle, finch and sparrow
Swift and flicker, hummer whirs.

Queedle queedle, wicka wicka
Cheer-up cheer-up, o-ka-leee.
Jay to warbler, blackbird, bunting
Sweeta sweeta, chee chee chee.

Chippa chippa, waxwing, starling
Kitter kitter, chip chip chip.
Weet weet chicka, tee-bit tweedle
Grackle, nuthatch, *kip kip kip.*

Cheep chip chippa, tuck tuck twitter
Bluebird, swallow, heed the call,
Delight this day that God has made!
Rejoice! Rejoice! One and all!

Barbara Davis-Pyles

44

TOGETHER

Stars and stones and butterflies,
bears and honeybees,
Sun and moon and meadowlands,
pebbles, pearls and trees.
Mountain mist and whales of blue
in tossing, turning seas
are all a part of nature,
and you're a part of these.

Carol Murray

45

WILDLIFE DELIGHT

A cardinal
dances,
rabbit
frolics,
squirrel
gathers,
deer grazes,
hawk circles,
raccoon scurries,
red-winged
blackbird
chirps,
all
creatures
of our
world.

Bobbie Saunders

SONG OF PRAISE

For all that dwell below the skies
Let songs of hope and faith arise
Let peace, goodwill on earth be sung
    Or barked or howled by every tongue!

LoraKim Joyner

IT IS A BEAUTIFUL WORLD

Above, above
All birds in air

Below, below
All earth's flowers

Inland, inland
All forest trees

Seaward, seaward
All ocean fish

Sing out and say
Again the refrain

"Behold this lovely world."

Mary Kawena Pukui

I AM THE FISH

I throw myself to the left.
I turn myself to the right.
I am the fish
Who glides in the water, who glides,
Who twists himself, who leaps.
Everything lives, everything dances, everything sings.

Author unknown, but commonly attributed to a Native African

ALL ANIMALS BELONG

Spirit of Life, help me remember
that all animals belong.
Bless the bats for eating mosquitoes.
Bless the crows and buzzards
for cleaning up the dead,
and bless even the snakes,
who keep the mice out of the rice.
Each of them is important.
And each does good in its own way.
Blessed be.

Eliza Blanchard

THIS LITTLE BEETLE

This little whirligig went to the pond.
This little lightning beetle stayed home.
This little lady beetle ate aphids.
This little stag beetle had none.
And this little June beetle went
buzz, buzz, buzz all the way home!

Diane Geiser

FOR FLYING THINGS

You gave us butterflies to dance
On rays of morning sun,
And katydids who loudly chirp
When summer days are done.
You sent the twinkling fireflies
To light the gentle night
And bumblebees with yellow coats
To kiss the flowers bright.
You created dragonflies
That dart about the sky.
Thank you, God, for all these things
That make my spirit fly.

Sandra E. McBride

HONEYBEE

Sweet creator.
   Pollinator.
Collect your nectar,
   save for later.

Matt Forrest Esenwine

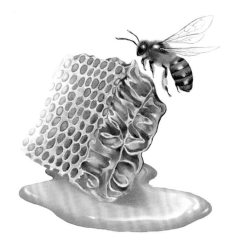

PRAY FOR US

mantis
in tall weeds

green prayer
in a green
cathedral

Jeanne Shannon

HARMLESS

Sometimes shy and humble
are God's smaller creatures
like a little green garden snake—
harmless

Often shy and humble
but sometimes funny, too,
is a tiny creeping inch worm—
harmless

Also shy and humble
living in a quiet corner
is that tangled daddy long legs—
harmless

Hilda Sanderson

FEATHER OR FUR

When you watch for
Feather or fur
Feather or fur
Do not stir
Do not stir.

Feather or fur
Come crawling
Creeping
Some come peeping
Some by night
And some by day.
Most come gently
All come softly
Do not scare
A friend away.

When you watch for
Feather or fur
Feather or fur
Do not stir
Do not stir.

John Becker

57

HYMN

coyote sends
her song
spiraling
past sand
and saguaros—

she, too,
knows who
swirled the sky
with stars,

who sent
the wind
to carry
her voice
across centuries

Irene Latham

58

ASK THE ANIMALS

But ask the animals, and they will teach you . . .
—Job 12:7

Ask the horse—
How to run swiftly.

Ask the eagle—
How to fly proudly.

Ask the whale—
How to swim deeply.

Ask the sparrow—
How to sing sweetly.

Ask the firefly—
How to shine brightly.

Mike W. Blottenberger

SEASONS

PSALM OF PRAISE

Sing for joy in summer
When earth is bright and green.
Sing with fun in winter
When snow is velveteen.
In spring sing out with gusto
For the life to soon unfold—
And sing with zest in autumn
For the woodlands colored gold.

Joan Stephen

SPRING

I'm shouting
I'm singing
I'm swinging through trees
I'm winging sky-high
With the buzzing black bees.
I'm the sun
I'm the moon
I'm the dew on the rose.
I'm a rabbit
Whose habit
Is twitching his nose.
I'm lively
I'm lovely
I'm kicking my heels.
I'm crying, "Come dance"
To the freshwater eels.
I'm racing through meadows
Without any coat.
I'm a gamboling lamb
I'm a light leaping goat
I'm a bud
I'm a bloom
I'm a dove on the wing.
I'm running on rooftops
And welcoming spring!

Karla Kuskin

AN EARTH SONG

It's an earth song—
And I've been waiting long
For an earth song.
It's a spring song!
I've been waiting long
For a spring song:
    Strong as the bursting of young buds,
    Strong as the shoots of a new plant,
    Strong as the coming of the first child
    From its mother's womb—
An earth song!
A body song!
A spring song!
And I've been waiting long
For an earth song.

Langston Hughes

64

SURPRISE

Summer pops
like a green balloon,
fresh as cheese,
full as the moon.
Branches that were
black and bare
just last week
are green and fair:
dogwood white
magnolia pink
apple dapple
and I think
nothing comes
with such surprise
as summer, summer,
blue jay skies.

Barbara Crooker

GOD'S POEMS

There is joy in a fountain
And joy in the hills;
I see it in the butterfly;
And gentle whip-poor-will.
The rivers, they are singing
With summer's rebirth;
For God's poems are all around
Filling our earth.

Marion Schoeberlein

66

JOHNNY APPLESEED GRACE

Oh, the Lord is good to me,
And so I thank the Lord,
For giving me the things I need:
The sun, the rain and the apple seed.
Oh, the Lord is good to me.

John Chapman, also known as Johnny Appleseed

NATURE CHANGES

I walk open-eyed in the wood.
Things sure change in the fall
And all that surrounds me is good.

From the long-dead log that once stood,
Grows a fir seedling, small.
I walk open-eyed in the wood.

I breathe deeply, wish I could
Blow this fresh air to all.
I walk open-eyed in the wood,
And all that's inside me is good.

Carol L. MacKay

THE SNOW CLOUDS KNOW

What's born above will soon be gone
to comfort what it falls upon.
Beauty blooms before the dawn;
this the snow clouds know.

Limbs are weak; snow is strong.
Days are short; nights are long.
Coyote sings a lonesome song;
this the snow clouds know.

Matt Forrest Esenwine

70

EACH SHADOW
HAS ITS SUNSHINE

Each shadow has its sunshine.
Each rainbow has its rain.
Each sunrise has its sunset
So it can come again.

Each songbird has its silence.
Each nighttime has its day.
Each thorn bush has its rosebud.
Each December has its May.

Each beginning has its ending.
Each ending has its start.
Each comes and goes because it knows
Each has a counterpart.

Charles Ghigna

71

CARDINAL

You're a beautiful present
on this winter day—
a flicker of red
in snow-filled pines,
like God painted
joy on earth.

Nancy Tupper Ling

72

CARING
FOR OUR
WORLD

IN MY DREAM

In my dream I save the planet,
the skies, the earth, and the sea.
I plant milkweed for the butterflies,
and zinnias for the bees.
I turn the soil with our compost,
and leave a blanket of leaves for all the snakes.
I never step on an ant,
and I leave spider webs alone.
I pick up my trash on the beach,
and I ride my bike when I can.
In my dream I gather all my friends,
and together we save the earth.

Judy Ackley Brown

EARTH'S VOICE

Listen!
The voice of the earth is calling,
    calling to you and to me.
"Speak out," it whispers,
"Speak for the open prairies and deserts,
    the rolling mountains, valleys, and hills.
Speak of their bounty and beauty
    season to season.
Speak out for oceans, lakes, rivers, and streams.
Speak of their boundless energy,
    their current and course through time.
Speak out for plants and animals.
Speak of their fragile lives
    so dependent on balance.
Speak of choice
    and respect and appreciation.
Speak of love and life.
Speak out!"

Theresa Mary Grass

I LOVE YOU, EARTH!

Jump from rocks.
Gather pinecones.
Smile at bugs.
Land on leaves.
Twirl through grass.
Splash in puddles.
Whisper,
Sing,
Shout,
"I love you, Earth!"

Barbara Younger

QUESTION

As asphalt and concrete
Replace bushes and trees,
As highways and buildings
Replace marshes and woods,
What will replace
The song of the birds?

Tony Chen

78

SAYING THANK YOU

Thank you for the little birds
and thank you for the flowers.
Thank you for the rain.

Thank you for the earth and seasons,
the rainbows and the moon,
and thank you for the trees that grow
both morning, night and noon.

Thank you for my friends and family,
and for snowflakes in the sky.
Thank you for the sun
and clouds slowly drifting by.

Magie Dominic

WHENEVER YOU SEE A TREE

Think
how many long years
this tree waited as a seed
for an animal or bird or wind or rain
to maybe carry it to maybe the right spot
where again it waited months for seasons to change
until time and temperature were fine enough to coax it
to swell and burst its hard shell so it could send slender roots
to clutch at grains of soil and let tender shoots reach toward the sun.
Think how many decades or centuries it thickened and climbed and grew
taller and deeper never knowing if it would find enough water or light
or when conditions would be right so it could keep on spreading leaves
adding blossoms and dancing.
Next time
you see
a tree
think
how
much
hope
it holds.

Padma Venkatraman

80

WHAT ARE WE DRAWING?

The Earth is God's paper.
You and I are the crayons.
Will you help me draw a picture—
so clever and colorful
that people smile
when they see it?

Kathleen Whitman Plucker

WHEN YOU PLANT A TREE

When you plant a tree,
A song begins.
It rises and grows
On tomorrow's wings.

Give the tree some love,
Some rain and sun,
And in its branches the birds
Will sing for everyone.

Mike W. Blottenberger

82

YOUR BUDDY TREE

Celebrate the trees of the world with your own Buddy Tree!
Choose a tree in your yard or a nearby location.

1. Give your Buddy Tree a name.
2. Learn what kind of tree it is.
3. Say, "I love you" with a hug.
4. Bring your tree a drink of water.
5. Tie a festive ribbon around its trunk.
6. Leave your tree a nature gift of a rock or flower.
7. Enjoy a snack under your tree.
8. Color or paint a picture of your tree.
9. Have someone take your picture by your tree.
10. Bring friends to meet your Buddy Tree.

Barbara Younger

FEEDING BIRDS
FROM YOUR HAND

Have you ever fed birds right from your hand?
It's super easy to do!
First, go to a park with your family,
one with plenty of trails and trees.
Hike on trails while listening for bird chatter
and looking for busy birds.
Then stretch out your hand, palm-side up,
and fingers together. Stand still as a statue.
Have a parent pour a mix of bird seed
and raw nuts onto your palm.
Then wait for your feathered friends to come.
Before you know it, they will!
Don't be surprised if they tickle your palm.
They usually do.
Happy bird feeding!

Joan Marie Arbogast

HURT NO LIVING THING

Hurt no living thing:
    Ladybird, nor butterfly
Nor moth with dusty wing,
    Nor cricket chirping cheerily,
Not grasshopper so light of leap,
    Nor dancing gnat, nor beetle fat,
Nor harmless worms that creep.

Christina Rossetti

LISTEN

Awaken ears
God is singing
in the melodies of birds
in the laughter of water.
Listen!

Awaken hearts
God is speaking
in the murmur of the wind
in the sigh of the willows
God whispers your name.
Listen!

Mary Lenore Quigley

I have learned you are never too small
to make a difference.

Greta Thunberg

I TAKE CARE OF THE EARTH

When I leave my room, I turn off the light.
When I brush my teeth, I don't waste water.
When I'm finished with paper, I recycle it.
When I eat an orange, I compost the peel.
When I go to the store, I bring my own bag.
Whenever I can, I take care of the Earth!

Barbara Younger

The earth is what we all have in common.

Wendell Berry

MOTHER EARTH IS MY HOME

The blue sky, her roof
shingled with clouds.
The tall forest timbers, her walls.
My feet love to walk on her carpet of moss.
This wonderful earth is my home.

The mountains, her back yard
winding with trails.
A sweet gentle rainfall, her shower.
My arms love to splash in her oceans and lakes.
This incredible earth is my home.

The gardens, her kitchen
growing our food.
She cares for her loved ones so well.
My body grows strong on all she provides.
This generous earth is my home.

The full moon, her night light
to rooms unexplored.
I smile as she tucks me into bed.
My heart feels so peaceful, asleep in her arms.
I'm blessed, Mother Earth is my home.

Cathy Stenquist

DEAR GOD,

Do stars shine because the night has eyes?
Is there a heaven and why do birds fly?
What is a cloud and do angels have wings?
Why do people cry and why do bees sting?
Do you have the answers so I could know?
Growing up is hard and I have far to go.
What is forever and who will I be?
Where is Oz and are there rainbows for me?
What is love and why do leaves fall?
Do you have a phone so I could call?
Do you have the answers so I could know?
Growing up is hard, God, and I have far to go.

Love,
Every Child

Judith A. Lindberg

90

IT'S UP TO US

It's up to us to make a difference,
yes, it's up to you and me
to care for the gifts we're given,
the earth, the sky, the sea.

It's up to us to celebrate
the sunshine and the rain,
to rejoice in each spring's promise
that flowers will bloom again.

It's up to us to treasure
pink skies of morning light,
sunsets bathed in purple
and twinkling stars at night.

It's up to us to count our blessings,
the beauty of our earth,
the miracles of nature and
each tiny creature's worth.

Susanne Wiggins Bunch

PERMISSION CREDITS

Joan Marie Arbogast, "Feeding Birds from Your Hand," reprinted by permission of the author.

Michelle Heidenrich Barnes, "Bedtime," reprinted by permission of the author.

Keri Biron, "Singing Stars," reprinted by permission of the author.

Eliza Blanchard, "All Animals Belong," reprinted by permission of the author.

Mike W. Blottenberger, "Ask the Animals" and "When You Plant a Tree," reprinted by permission of the author.

Judy Ackley Brown, "I Love to Wonder!" and "In My Dream," reprinted by permission of the author.

Susanne Wiggins Bunch, "A Child's Lullaby for Earth," "It's Up to Us," and "Rainforest Symphony," reprinted by permission of the author.

Janine Canan, "I Am the Earth," reprinted by permission of June Cotner.

Tony Chen, "Question" from *All the Wild Wonders*, written by Wendy Cooling and illustrated by Piet Grobler, published by Frances Lincoln Children's Books, an imprint of The Quarto Group, copyright © 2012. Reproduced by permission of Quarto Publishing PLC.

Barbara Crooker, "Surprise," originally published in *Shoofly*, 1994, reprinted by permission of the author.

Barbara Davis-Pyles, "Morning Song," reprinted by permission of the author.

Corrine De Winter, "Earth Speaks" and "Magical Forest," reprinted by permission of the author.

Magie Dominic, "Saying Thank You," reprinted by permission of the author.

Nancy Engler, "Stony Wonders," reprinted by permission of the author.

Matt Forrest Esenwine, "Honeybee" and "The Snow Clouds Know," reprinted by permission of the author.

Aileen Fisher, "Hard to Believe" from *Sing of Earth and Sky*, copyright © 2001 by Aileen Lucia Fisher. Published by Wordsong, an imprint of Astra Publishing House, New York, USA. All rights reserved. Reprinted by permission of Astra Publishing House, Ltd.

John Foster, "Inside a Shell" from *The Works 8,* copyright © 1989 by John Foster. Published by Macmillan Children's Books. Reprinted by permission of the author.

Diane Geiser, "This Little Beetle," reprinted by permission of the author.

Charles Ghigna, "Each Shadow Has Its Sunshine," "Life Cycle," and "Think Like a River," reprinted by permission of the author.

Theresa Mary Grass, "Earth's Voice," reprinted by permission of the author.

LoraKim Joyner, "Song of Praise," reprinted by permission of the author.

Karla Kuskin, "Spring" from *In the Middle of the Trees*, copyright © 1959, renewed 1986 by Karla Kuskin. Reprinted by permission of S©ott Treimel NY.

Irene Latham, "Hymn," reprinted by permission of the author.

Fanny M. Levin, "Purple," reprinted by permission of the author.

Judith A. Lindberg, "Dear God," reprinted by permission of the author.

Nancy Tupper Ling, "Bless the Earth" and "Cardinal," reprinted by permission of the author.

Daphne Lister, "The Sea's Treasures," reprinted by permission of Joe Peters.

Jill Noblit MacGregor, "Everyday Wonders" and "Incredible Creation," reprinted by permission of the author.

Carol L. MacKay, "Nature Changes," reprinted by permission of the author.

Sandra E. McBride, "For Flying Things," reprinted by permission of the author.

Barbara J. Mitchell, "Dreams for My World," reprinted by permission of the author.

Carol Murray, "Think Tenderly of Me" and "Together," reprinted by permission of the author.

Jillian Pappan, "If I Could See the Sky," reprinted by permission of the author.

Kathleen Whitman Plucker, "What Are We Drawing?," reprinted by permission of the author.

Mary Kawena Pukui, "It Is a Beautiful World" ("He Nani Ke Ao Nei") from *The Penguin Book of Oral Poetry,* copyright © 1978. Reprinted by permission of Laʻakea Suganuma, on behalf of The Mary Kawena Pukui Cultural Preservation Society.

Mary Lenore Quigley, "Listen," reprinted by permission of the author.

Hilda Sanderson, "Harmless," reprinted by permission of the author.

Bobbie Saunders, "Wildlife Delight," reprinted by permission of the author.

Marion Schoeberlein, "God's Poems," reprinted by permission of Sherry Jungwirth.

Jeanne Shannon, "Pray for Us," reprinted by permission of the author.

Charlotte Sheer, "Dear Creator," reprinted by permission of the author.

Joyce Sidman, "Hello, Earth!" from *Hello, Earth!,* published by Eerdmans Books for Young Readers, an imprint of Wm B. Eerdmans Publishing Co., Grand Rapids, MI. Reprinted by permission of Wm. B. Eerdmans Publishing Co.

Amanda Smith, "Wonder," reprinted by permission of the author.

Cathy Stenquist, "Mother Earth Is My Home," reprinted by permission of the author.

Joan Stephen, "Psalm of Praise," reprinted by permission of Jan Jadlowski.

Ramnath Subramanian, "Magic Box," reprinted by permission of the author.

Padma Venkatraman, "Whenever You See a Tree," reprinted by permission of the author.

Barbara Younger, "Bravo, World!," "I Love You, Earth!," "I Take Care of the Earth," and "Your Buddy Tree," reprinted by permission of the author.

AUTHOR INDEX

ABOUT THE EDITORS

JUNE COTNER is the author of thirty-eight books, including the bestselling *Graces* (HarperOne), *Bedside Prayers* (HarperOne), and *House Blessings* (Chronicle Books). Her newest children's book is *For Every Little Thing: Poems and Prayers to Celebrate the Day* (Eerdmans Young Readers), co-authored with Nancy Tupper Ling. June's books altogether have sold more than one million copies and have been featured in many national publications, including *USA Today, Better Homes & Gardens, Woman's Day, Family Circle,* and *The Wall Street Journal.* June has appeared on national television and radio programs.

In 2011, June adopted Indy, a chocolate lab/Doberman mix (a LabraDobie!), from the Freedom Tails program at Stafford Creek Corrections Center in Aberdeen, Washington. She and Indy have appeared on the television shows *AM Northwest* (Portland, Oregon) and *New Day Northwest* (Seattle).

A graduate of the University of California at Berkeley, June is the mother of two grown children and lives in Poulsbo, Washington, with her husband. Her hobbies include hiking and creating wilderness reels on Instagram.

For more information, please visit June's website at www.junecotner.com.

NANCY TUPPER LING is a children's author, poet, and librarian. She has great fun teaching poetry to grade-school children, high school students, fellow poets, and senior citizens. Her picture books include *Double Happiness* (Chronicle Books), *My Sister, Alicia May* (Pleasant St. Press), *The Story I'll Tell* (Lee & Low Books), *The Yin-Yang Sisters and the Dragon Frightful* (Penguin Young Readers), and her latest, *For Every Little Thing: Poems and Prayers to Celebrate the Day* (Eerdmans Young Readers), co-authored with June Cotner.

With June, Nancy also co-authored two anthologies for adults titled *Toasts: The Perfect Words to Celebrate Every Occasion* (Viva Editions) and *Family Celebrations: Poems, Toasts, and Traditions for Every Occasion* (Andrews McMeel Publishing).

Her books received starred reviews from *Kirkus* and *Publishers Weekly*, as well as a 2016 Massachusetts Book Award and an honorable mention from the Boston Authors Club. Nancy was the winner of the *Writer's Digest* Grand Prize for her poem "White Birch."

In 2002 she founded the Fine Line Poets. She has served as poetry judge and library liaison for the Massachusetts State Poetry Society. For more information, visit her websites at www.nancytupperling.com and www.finelinepoets.com.

Published in the United States by Convergent Books, an imprint of
Random House, a division of Penguin Random House LLC, New York.

Convergent Books is a registered trademark and the
Convergent colophon is a trademark of Penguin Random House LLC.

Permission credits are located on pages 92–93.

ISBN 978-0-593-57766-0
Ebook ISBN 978-0-593-57767-7

The Cataloging-in-Publication Data
is on file with the Library of Congress.

Printed in China

convergentbooks.com

10 9 8 7 6 5 4 3 2 1

First Edition

Book and cover design by Ashley Tucker

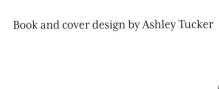